Learn to Crochet

This book is a revised edition of old Paragon books No 6 and C126 (Learn to Crochet), originally published by Paragon Art Needlecraft Pty Ltd, Sydney, NSW. Learn to crochet instructions in this edition have been expanded and simplified. Diagrams have been provided for both left and right handed crocheters. Some of the original patterns that were too complicated or outdated have been omitted. Included are doily patterns from C134 (Popcorn Rings Tablecloth) and Book 2 (Crochet Notions). Craft Moods is now the copyright owner and publisher for all Paragon publications.

Edited by: Vicki Moodie.

Copyright: R & V Moodie   1998

GW00602735

All rights reserved. Except as provided under the copyright act, no part of this book may be reproduced in any form or by any means, including photocopying, without permission in writing from the publisher.

ISBN 1 876373 05 9

Published by

CRAFT MOODS
P.O. Box 1096
CABOOLTURE Qld. 4510
Australia

Phone/Fax (07) 5496 6826
www.craftmoods.com.au

Printed by   NICHOLSON PRINTERS Pty Ltd
6C 43 Industrial Avenue
Morayfield Road
CABOOLTURE Qld. 4510

Phone (07) 5495 1371
Fax (07) 5498 3783

2/00

CONTENTS

ABBREVIATIONS

blk	block	quintr	quintuple treble
ch	chain	sl st	slip stitch
dc	double crochet	sp(s)	space(es)
dtr	double treble	st(s)	stitch(es)
htr	half treble	tr	treble
quadtr	quadruple treble	triptr	triple treble

GENERAL INSTRUCTIONS

This book is intended as an instructional book which should be used as a whole, and not in part. Each instruction will continue from the previous one, therefore read from the beginning carefully and master each step before continuing onto the next.

Some of the instructions in this book may vary from instructions found in other books. This does not mean that either way is incorrect, but simply a variation of each other. Over the years I have found my variation to be the easiest way for a beginner to learn, even if you are a left hander.

The illustrations on pages 5 to 7 are for right handed pupils only, and *the illustrations on pages 8 to 10 are for left handed pupils only.*

Illustrations of stitches on pages 11 to 21, are set out as follows:

The instructions for each stitch apply to both right and *left handed* pupils.

The right hand side illustrations are for right handed pupils, and *the left hand side illustrations are for left handed pupils.*

To avoid confusion, we suggest you use a plain sheet of paper to cover the illustrations on the side not required.

All crochet stitches are based on the action of a loop pulled through another loop with a hook. When crocheting, right handed pupils work from right to left and *left handed pupils work from left to right.*

When learning the basic steps, begin with 8ply yarn and a 3.50mm hook OR 4ply yarn and a 2.50mm hook, so that each stitch is clearly visible. Practise the simple steps first before attempting the finer threads.

In all crocheting, pick up the two top threads of each stitch unless otherwise stated.

CHAIN (ch) is the basis of all crocheting. Chain is used to begin crocheting, to obtain height at the beginning of a row, and in patterns where an opening or a hole is required. When crocheting the starting row (foundation chain), work the chain stitches more loosely than the following rows.

CROCHET THREADS

Texture plays an important part in the beauty of crochet. The finer mercerised threads are more effective for delicate designs used for tablecloths, doilies and edges. However for some of us, if seeing and grasping the thread is a little challenging, work in a larger thread such as #10, or 4ply cotton. The crocheted items will be larger so this will have to be taken into account. Also consider that different brands or colours of the same size thread may vary in thickness.

Avoid joining the thread in the middle of a pattern and never make knots to join the thread. As the thread is coming to an end, place the new thread along the top of the work and crochet a few stitches over this. Before the old thread has run out, change to the new thread and work the stitches over the old thread. Cut off or weave in any ends that are left.

CROCHET HOOKS

Crochet hooks are made of steel, plastic and alloy metals. Each hook is used with a set size of thread unless otherwise stated in the pattern. A pattern should specify a hook size and a tension, so a larger or smaller hook may be required to achieve that tension. If the crocheting is too loose, use a smaller hook, if the crocheting is too tight, use a larger hook. The table below is to be used as a guide only for thread and hook size.

Thread	Hook
#80 & #100	0.60mm
#60	0.75mm
#40	1.00mm
#20	1.25mm
#10	1.50mm - 1.75mm
3ply	2.00mm - 2.50mm
4ply	2.50mm - 3.00mm
8ply	3.50mm - 4.00mm

Old	New	Old	New
6	0.60	9	3.50
5	0.75	8	4.00
4	1.00	7	4.50
3	1.25	6	5.00
2½	1.50	5	5.50
2	1.75	4	6.00
14	2.00	2	7.00
12	2.50		
11	3.00		

HOW TO CROCHET RIGHT HANDED

STEP 1.
TO MAKE A LOOP

1. Grasp the thread near the end between the thumb and the forefinger of the left hand.

2. With the right hand, make a loop by lapping the long thread over the short thread.

3. Hold this loop in place between the thumb and the forefinger of the left hand (Fig 1).

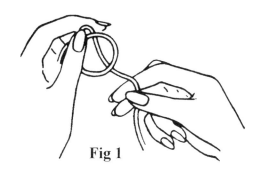

Fig 1

STEP 2.
1. With the right hand, take hold of the broad bar of the hook as you would a pencil.

2. Insert the hook through the loop and under the long thread. With the right hand, catch the long end of the thread (Fig 2). Draw the loop through.

3. Do not remove the hook from the thread.

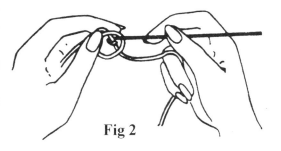

Fig 2

STEP 3.
1. Pull the short end and the ball thread in opposite directions to bring the loop around the end of the hook, but not too tight (Fig 3).

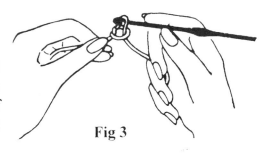

Fig 3

STEP 4.
WHAT TO DO WITH THE LEFT HAND

1. Measure with your eye about 10cm along the ball thread from the loop on the hook.

2. At about this point, insert the thread between the ring finger and the little finger, having the palm of the hand facing up (Fig 4).

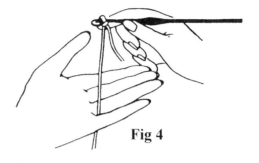

Fig 4

STEP 5.

1. Bring the thread towards the back, under the little finger and the ring finger, over the middle finger and under the forefinger towards the thumb (Fig 5).

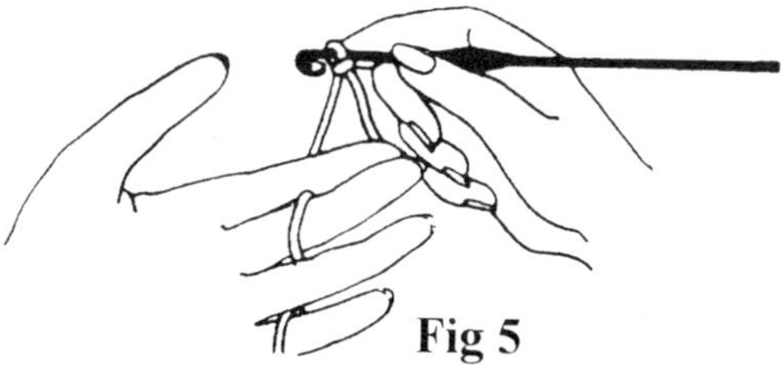

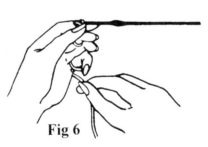

Fig 5

STEP 6.

1. Grasp the hook and the loop between the thumb and the forefinger of the left hand.

2. Gently pull the ball thread so that it lies around the fingers firmly, but not tightly (Fig 6).

3. Catch the knot of the loop between the thumb and the forefinger.

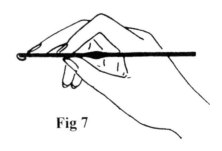

Fig 6

STEP 7.
WHAT TO DO WITH THE RIGHT HAND

1. Take hold of the broad bar of the hook as you would a pencil.

2. Bring the middle finger forward to rest near the tip of the hook (Fig. 7).

Fig 7

STEP 8.

1. Adjust the fingers of the left hand as in Fig 8 - the middle finger is bent to regulate the tension, the ring and the little fingers control the thread. The motion of the hook in the right hand and the thread in the left hand should be free and even. Ease comes with practice.

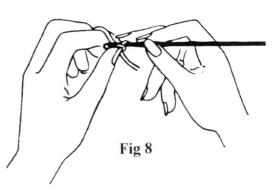

Fig 8

STEP 9.

CHAIN (ch)

1. Pass the hook under the thread and catch the thread with the hook. This is called **"thread over"** or yarn over hook (Fig 9).

2. Draw the thread through the loop on the hook. This makes one **chain (ch).**

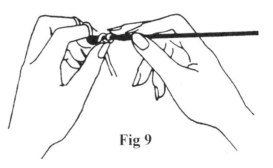

Fig 9

STEP 10.

1. Repeat Step 9 until you have as many chain (ch) as you need - one loop always remains on the hook (Fig 10).

2. Always keep the thumb and the forefinger of the left hand near the stitch on which you are working.

3. Practise making chain stitches until they are even in size.

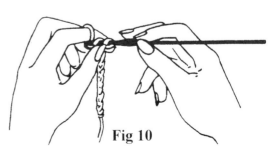

Fig 10

HOW TO CROCHET LEFT HANDED

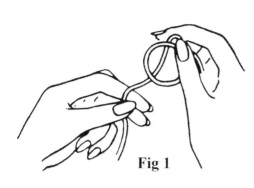

Fig 1

STEP 1.
TO MAKE A LOOP
1. Grasp the thread near the end between the thumb and the forefinger of the right hand.
2. With the left hand make a loop by lapping the long thread over the short thread.
3. Hold the loop in place between the thumb and the forefinger of the right hand (Fig 1).

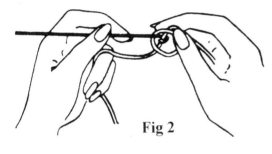

Fig 2

STEP 2.
1. With the left hand, take hold of the broad bar of the hook as you would a pencil.
2. Insert the hook through the loop and under the long thread. With the left hand catch the long end of the thread (Fig 2). Draw the loop through.
3. Do not remove the hook from the thread.

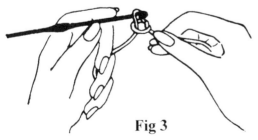

Fig 3

STEP 3.
1. Pull the short end and the ball thread in opposite directions to bring the loop around the end of the hook, but not too tight (Fig 3).

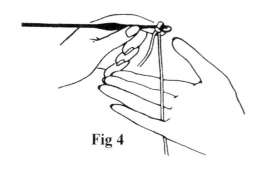

Fig 4

STEP 4.
WHAT TO DO WITH THE RIGHT HAND

1. Measure with your eye about 10cm along the ball thread from the loop on the hook.

2. At about this point, insert the thread between the ring finger and the little finger, having the palm of the hand facing up (Fig 4).

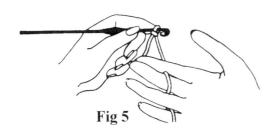

Fig 5

STEP 5.

1. Bring the thread towards the back, under the little finger and the ring finger, over the middle finger and under the forefinger towards the thumb (Fig 5).

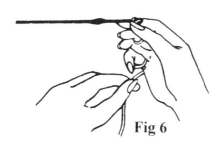

Fig 6

STEP 6.

1. Grasp the hook and the loop between the thumb and the forefinger of the right hand.

2. Gently pull the ball thread so that it lies around the fingers firmly, but not tightly (Fig 6).

3. Catch the knot of the loop between the thumb and the forefinger.

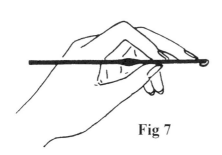

Fig 7

STEP 7.
WHAT TO DO WITH THE LEFT HAND

1. Take hold of the broad bar of hook as you would a pencil.

2. Bring the middle finger forward to rest near the tip of the hook (Fig 7).

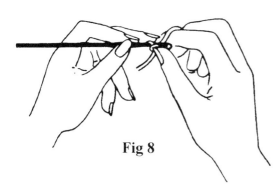

Fig 8

STEP 8.

1. Adjust the fingers of the right hand as in Fig 8 - the middle finger is bent to regulate the tension, the ring and the little fingers control the thread. The motion of the hook in the left hand and the thread in the right hand should be free and even. Ease comes with practice.

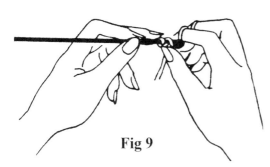

Fig 9

STEP 9.

CHAIN (ch)

1. Pass the hook under the thread and catch the thread with the hook. This is called **"thread over"** or yarn over hook (Fig 9).

2. Draw the thread through the loop on the hook. This makes one **chain (ch).**

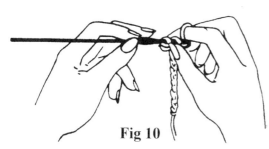

Fig 10

STEP 10.

1. Repeat Step 9 until you have as many chain (ch) as you need - one loop always remains on the hook (Fig 10).

2. Always keep the thumb and the forefinger of the right hand near the stitch on which you are working.

3. Practise making chain stitches until they are even in size.

SLIP STITCH (sl st)

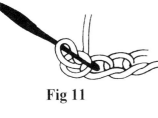

Fig 11

Fig 11

Slip stitching is used to move across the row without creating depth and to join rounds in circular crocheting.

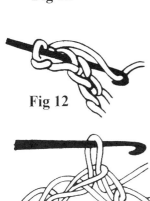

Fig 12

Fig 12

Make a length of chain, insert the hook from the front, under the two top threads of the stitch next to the hook (Fig 11), thread over (Fig 12), and draw it through the stitch AND the loop on the hook in one movement. Repeat across the row of chain (Fig 13).

Fig 13

Fig 13

DOUBLE CROCHET (dc)

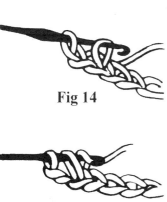

Fig 14

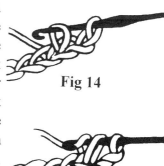

Fig 14

Make a length of chain, insert the hook from the front, under the two top threads of the chain next to the hook (Fig 11), thread over (Fig 12), and draw it through the ch. There are now two loops on the hook (Fig 14), thread over (Fig 15), and draw through the two loops, one loop

Fig 15

Fig 15

will remain on the hook. One double crochet (1dc) now completed. (Fig 16)

For next dc, insert the hook under the two top threads of the next stitch and repeat as before.

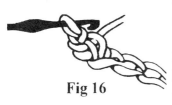

Fig 16

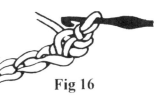

Fig 16

HALF TREBLE (htr)

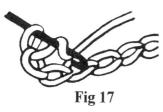

Fig 17

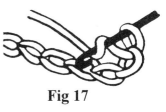

Fig 17

Make a length of chain, thread over, insert the hook from the front, under the two top threads of the 3rd ch from the hook (Fig 17), thread over, and draw it through this ch. There are now three loops on the hook, thread over (Fig 18), and draw it through all three loops, one loop will remain on the hook.
One half treble (1htr) completed (Fig 19).

For the next htr, thread over, insert the hook under the two top threads of the next ch and repeat as before.

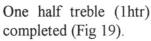

Fig 18

Fig 18

Fig 19

Fig 19

TREBLE (tr)

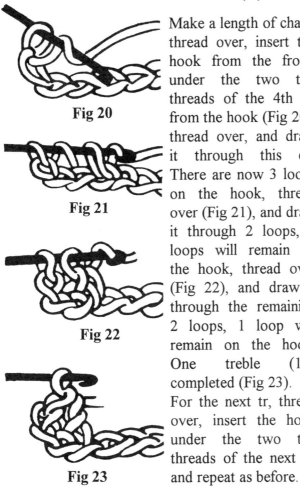

Fig 20

Fig 21

Fig 22

Fig 23

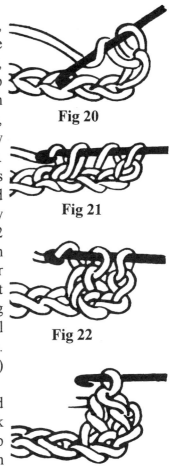

Fig 20

Fig 21

Fig 22

Fig 23

Make a length of chain, thread over, insert the hook from the front, under the two top threads of the 4th ch from the hook (Fig 20), thread over, and draw it through this ch. There are now 3 loops on the hook, thread over (Fig 21), and draw it through 2 loops, 2 loops will remain on the hook, thread over (Fig 22), and draw it through the remaining 2 loops, 1 loop will remain on the hook. One treble (1tr) completed (Fig 23).

For the next tr, thread over, insert the hook under the two top threads of the next ch and repeat as before.

DOUBLE TREBLE (dtr)

Make a length of chain, thread over twice, insert the hook from the front, under the two top threads of the 5th ch from the hook, thread over, and draw it through the ch. There are now 4 loops on the hook, thread over, and draw it through 2 loops, 3 loops will remain on the hook, thread over again, and draw it through 2 loops, 2 loops will remain on the hook, thread over again, and draw it through the remaining 2 loops, 1 loop will remain on the hook. One double treble (1dtr) now

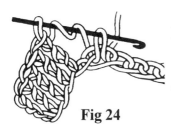

Fig 24

completed.
For next dtr, thread over twice, insert the hook under the two top threads of the next ch and repeat as before (Fig 24).

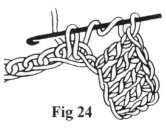

Fig 24

TRIPLE TREBLE (triptr)

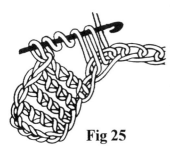

Fig 25

Make a length of chain, thread over three times, insert the hook from the front, under the two top threads of the 6th ch from the hook, thread over, and draw it through the ch.

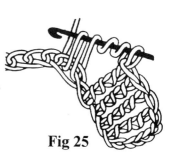

Fig 25

There are now 5 loops on the hook, thread over, and draw it through 2 loops, 4 loops will remain on the hook, thread over again, and draw it through 2 loops, 3 loops will remain on the hook, thread over again, and draw it through 2 loops, 2 loops will remain on the hook, thread over again, and draw it through the remaining 2 loops, 1 loop will remain on the hook. One triple treble (triptr) now completed.

For next triptr, thread over three times, insert the hook under the two top threads of the next ch and repeat as before (Fig 25).

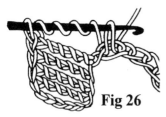

Fig 26

QUADRUPLE TREBLE (quadtr)

Make a length of chain, thread over four times,

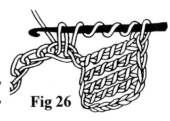

Fig 26

insert the hook from the front, under the two top threads of the 7th ch from the hook, thread over, and draw it through the ch. There are now 6 loops on the hook, thread over, and draw it through 2 loops, 5 loops will remain on the hook, thread over again, and draw it through 2 loops, 4 loops will remain on the hook, thread over again, and draw it through 2 loops, 3 loops will remain on the hook, thread over again, and draw it through 2 loops, 2 loops will remain on the hook, thread over again, and draw it through the remaining 2 loops, 1 loop will remain on the hook. One quadruple treble (1quadtr) now completed.

For the next quadtr, thread over four times, insert the hook under the two top threads of the next ch and repeat as before (Fig 26).

QUINTUPLE TREBLE (quintr)

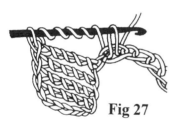

Make a length of chain, thread over five times, insert the hook from the front, under the two top threads of the 8th ch from the hook, thread over, and draw it through the ch.

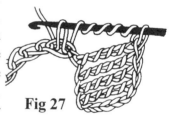

Fig 27

There are now 7 loops on the hook, thread over, and draw it through 2 loops, 6 loops will remain on the hook, thread over again, and draw it through 2 loops, 5 loops will remain on the hook, thread over again, and draw it through 2 loops, 4 loops will remain on the hook, thread over again, and draw it through 2 loops, 3 loops will remain on the hook, thread over again, and draw it through 2 loops, 2 loops will remain on the hook, thread over again, and draw it through the remaining 2 loops, 1 loop will remain on the hook. One quintuple treble (1quintr) now completed.

For next quintuple tr, thread over five times, insert the hook under the 2 top threads of the next ch and repeat as before (Fig 27).

HOW TO READ A PATTERN

If the pattern is written in rows, crochet the first row then turn the work, continue the next row to the end, turn the work again and then proceed with the 3rd and following rows, turning at the end of each row.

If the pattern is written in rounds, crochet the first round, ending with a slip stitch into the top of the beginning stitch of the round. DO NOT TURN the work between rounds.

When the instructions are inside a bracket, repeat them as many times as specified, for example (5ch, 1dc in next dc) 6 times, this means to work all in the brackets 6 times only.

An * (asterisk) in a pattern means that the instruction after the * is repeated as many times as specified, in addition to the original instruction that followed the asterisk. For example, (Miss 2tr, * 1tr in next tr, 5ch, repeat from * to last 1tr, 1tr in last tr), means to miss the first 2tr, then work the next 1tr and 5ch as stated, then continue to repeat them until 1tr remains, then work 1tr in the last tr.

INCREASING

Precise instructions for increasing are usually given in each pattern. However, a simple increase will consist of working 2 stitches (instead of one), into one stitch of the previous row. This may be done at either end of the row or in any part of the row. The pattern will usually specify the correct procedure.

DECREASING

When decreasing, the pattern will specify the method to be used.

"Miss one stitch" - miss the next stitch and work into the following stitch. This will decrease the number of stitches by one. Also referred to as "skip 1" in some patterns.

"Work 2sts tog" - This is achieved by not finishing either of the next 2 stitches, but leaving the last loop of each stitch on the hook in addition to the loop already on the hook. Thread over, and pull the yarn through all the loops to form 1 loop on the hook. This produces a less obvious space.

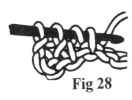

Fig 28

Fig 28

For example to "work 2sts tog" or decrease over treble, complete the first treble to the point where there are 2 loops on the hook. Work the next treble until there are 4 loops on the hook (Fig 28), thread over and draw the thread through 2 loops (Fig 29), thread over again and draw the thread through the remaining 3 loops. One loop remains on the hook. This is often referred to as treble decrease or decrease treble. (Fig 30)

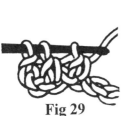

Fig 29

Fig 29

When decreasing at the beginning of a row, simply slip stitch over the required number of stitches to be decreased, then work the turning chain and continue the row.

Fig 30

Fig 30

When decreasing at the end of a row, work to within the number of stitches to be decreased, turn work and continue the next row.

Increases and decreases in stitches and changing the type of stitch are the basis of all patterns. For example, 1dc in next st, miss 2sts, 5tr in next st, miss 2sts, 1dc in next st (Fig 31), forms a shell design.

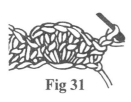

Fig 31

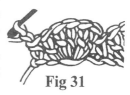

Fig 31

CROCHETING IN ROWS

Make a length of chain (foundation chain). Depending on the stitch to be used, extra chain will need to be added to form the height of the stitch. These chain count as the first stitch unless otherwise stated. Some patterns say to "miss" a certain number of stitches at the beginning of the first row. This also gives the required height. Use the table below as a guide.

When crocheting in rows, for example in trebles, work a foundation row and when the last

Fig 32

treble is completed, turn the work so that the reverse side is facing. Work 3 chain (turning chain) for height, and because the turning chain will count as the first stitch of this new row, miss the last worked stitch of

the previous row and work the next treble into the top of the next treble (Fig 32).

Fig 32

Remember to always insert the hook under the two top threads of each stitch, unless the pattern states otherwise.

Continue across the row. The last treble of the row will be worked into the top of the turning chain, that is, into the 3rd chain of the beginning 3ch of the last row.

Some patterns, in which the turning chain does not count as the first stitch at the beginning of the row, require you to work into the last stitch of the previous row, and in this case you do not work a stitch into the turning chain at the end of the row.

The turning chain table is used as a guide only when determining the number of stitches required for a turning chain. Depending on the type and texture of thread / yarn used, the number of chain can be varied. Similarly, rows of dc, htr, dtr, and other sts are worked,

varying the height of the turning chain.

Double crochet (dc) 1ch
Half treble (htr).....................2ch
Treble (tr) 3ch
Double treble (dtr) 4ch
Triple treble (triptr)..............5ch
Quadruple treble (quadtr)......6ch
Quintuple treble (quintr)........7ch

BREAK OFF is to finish off. Simply cut the thread about 8 - 10cm long. Bring the cut end through the last remaining loop on the hook and pull tightly (Figs 33 and 34). Weave this end back into the main part of the work with a blunt needle.

Fig 33

Fig 34

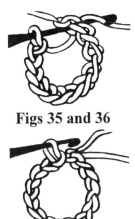

Figs 35 and 36

TO CROCHET IN ROUNDS

Figs 35 and 36

When crocheting in rounds, unless stated in the pattern, never turn the work between the rounds. Each stitch is still worked under the two top threads of the stitch in the previous round. A "right side" will be noticeable in the crocheted piece. Rounds are joined with a slip stitch (sl st) [Figs 35 and 36]. Rounds can be worked in a variety of stitches. The example below is worked in treble only.

To begin make 4ch. Join with a sl st into the first ch to form a ring. Do not twist the work.

Round 1. 3ch, (this is for height and will count as one st). Work 11 treble into the centre of the ring. Join the round with a sl st into the 3rd ch of the beginning 3ch. (12tr)

Round 2. 3ch, 1tr in same place as sl st, 2tr in each of the other tr, join the round with a sl st into the 3rd ch of the beginning 3ch. (24tr) This is increasing in every stitch.

In the next round the stitches must be increased evenly, so proceed as follows:

Round 3. 3ch, * 2tr in next tr, 1tr in the next tr; repeat from * to last st, 2tr in this st. Join the round with a sl st into the 3rd ch of the

beginning 3ch. (36tr) The increase was made in every second stitch.

Increasing is achieved by working a required number of stitches into one stitch. Most patterns state when to increase and the method to use. The aim is to increase at a rate that allows the crocheting to remain flat.

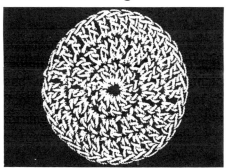

Variations of terminology:
"Round 1" may read "1st round", and "into the 3rd ch of the beginning 3ch" may read "into the top of the turning ch".

CLUSTERS AND POPCORNS

are commonly used in edges, motifs and patterns. Any number of stitches can be used and so can any combinations of any type of stitch. It is common for most patterns to use the one stitch for height.

CLUSTERS (cl)

A cluster may vary from two to six stitches. It may be worked over a given number of sts, into one stitch or into a space. Following are examples of these variations.

Fig 37

1. A 4dtr cluster over 4 stitches. Leaving the last loop of each stitch on the hook, work 1dtr into each of the following 4 stitches, thread over hook and draw it through all the remaining 5 loops on the hook (Fig 37).

Fig 37

Figs 38 and 39

2. A 3tr cluster worked into one stitch. Leaving the last loop of each stitch on the hook, work 3tr into the one stitch, thread over hook, pull through all 4 loops on the hook (Figs 38 and 39).

Figs 38 and 39

3. A 3dtr cluster worked into a space or loop. Leaving the last loop of each stitch on the hook, work 3dtr into the space of the previous row, thread over hook and draw it through all the remaining 4 loops on the hook (Fig 40).

Fig 40

Fig 40

POPCORN

Fig 41

A popcorn is a group of three or more stitches worked into the same stitch of the previous row and is completed as follows:

Fig 42

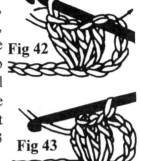

Fig 42

Fig 43

To make a 3tr popcorn. Work 3tr into the same stitch (Fig 41), remove the loop from the hook, insert the hook into the top of the first treble of this group, then into the loop just dropped (Fig 42), pull the loop through the first treble (Fig 43). A popcorn is usually, but not always, followed by 2 or 3 chain to define the popcorn.

Fig 43

FILET CROCHET is a technique based on forming designs with solid and open squares called blocks and spaces. This creates a lace net effect.

To make a space, miss 2sts, 2ch, 1tr in next stitch. The 2ch form the space and the 1tr completes the space, which is two stitches high and two stitches wide. A space is therefore 2ch 1tr.

A block is a group of treble stitches (usually three) which form the solid part of the design either side of the space.

Both blocks and spaces are worked over either a block or a space.

Fig 44 shows 3tr (block), 2ch 1tr (space), 3tr (block).

| block | space | block |

Fig 44

Double treble are also used in filet work but there would be 3ch instead of 2ch to form the space.

Filet designs are shown as a pattern of squares rather than words, as it is easier to follow.

The size of the design may be altered by using a different thickness of yarn other than that specified in the pattern.

EDGES

Edges may be worked directly onto the fabric, or worked onto a foundation chain and then sewn to the fabric at a later date. Edges can be worked lengthways or widthways depending on the pattern.

Three simple edges to try, each using #10 cotton and 1.75mm hook.

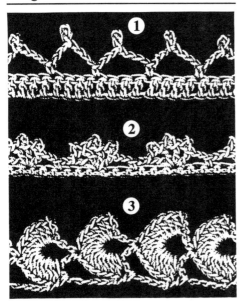

EDGE No 1. Picot. Requires a multiple of 4 stitches.
This edge is usually worked as the last row of an edge or onto a foundation row of dc, htr or tr.
1dc into first st, * 7ch, sl st into the 4th ch from the hook (picot made), 3ch, miss 3sts of the foundation row, 1dc in next st and repeat from * to end. Fasten off.

EDGE No 2. This edge is worked onto a foundation chain but could be worked directly onto a row of dc as the example shows.

Make a chain the desired length in (multiples of 6) + 2. (e.g. 20ch)

Row 1. Miss 1ch, 1dc in each ch to end, turn. (multiples of 6 + 1 dc)

Row 2. 1dc into the first dc, * 2ch, miss 2dc, into next dc work ([1tr 2ch 1dc into top of last tr] 3 times, 1tr), 2ch, miss 2dc, 1dc in next dc; repeat from * to end of row. (groups of [1tr 2ch 1dc] 3 times and 1tr, separated by 2ch 1dc 2ch.)
Fasten off.

EDGE No 3. This edge is worked widthways and sewn to the fabric later.

Make 6ch.

Row 1. 1tr into the 6th ch from the hook, 3ch, turn.

Row 2. (right side of work) 13tr in space just made, 7ch, turn.

Row 3. Miss 6tr, (1tr 5ch 1tr) into next tr, 3ch, turn.

Row 4. 13tr into the 5ch loop, 1tr into the turning 7ch loop, 7ch, turn.

Repeat rows 3 and 4 until the length required, omitting the 7ch in the very last row. Fasten off.

Other edges to try using a finer thread, #20 or #40.

EDGE No 4.

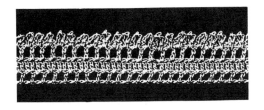

Make a length of chain, (multiples of 2) + 6.

Row 1. 1tr into 6th ch from hook, * 1ch, miss 1ch, 1tr into next ch; repeat from * until row is length required, 3ch, turn.

Row 2. 1tr into next 1ch sp, 1tr into next tr; repeat from * ending with 1tr into last sp, 1tr into top of turning ch, 4ch, turn.

Row 3. Miss first 2tr, 1tr into next tr, * 1ch, miss 1tr, 1tr into next tr; repeat from * ending with 1ch, miss 1tr, 1tr into top of turning ch, 1ch, turn.

Row 4. Into each sp work (1dc 5ch and 1dc). Fasten off.

EDGE No 5.

Make 11ch.

Row 1. Leaving the last loop of each st on the hook, work 3dtr into 11th ch from hook, thread over and pull through all loops on hook (a cluster made), 5ch, turn.

Row 2. 1tr into top of cluster, 10ch, turn.

Row 3. Make a 3dtr cluster into top of last tr, 5ch, turn.

Repeat 2nd and 3rd rows for length required, ending with a 3dtr cluster, 5ch.
Now work along the long edge containing the 5 ch loops as follows:
* Into next 5ch loop work (a 3dtr cluster 5ch and a 3dtr cluster); repeat from * to end, 5ch, sl st in base of beginning cluster.

Now work along opposite edge as follows:
* Into the 10ch loop work [(3dc, 3ch) 3 times and 3dc], 1dc in the space between the loops; repeat from * to end, ending 1dc in top of cluster. Fasten off.

EDGE No 6.

Make a length of chain (even multiples of 5) + 3.

Row 1. 1dc into 2nd ch from hook, * 5ch, 1dc into each of next 5ch; repeat from * ending with 5ch, 1dc into next ch (be sure to have an odd number of loops), turn.

Row 2. Sl st into the loop, 4ch, work a 2dtr cluster into same loop, 8ch, work a 3dtr cluster into same loop, * 3ch, 1dc into next loop, 3ch, into next loop work (a 3dtr cluster 8ch and a 3dtr cluster); repeat from * to end, 1ch, turn.

Row 3. * Into next 8ch loop work [(2dc 3ch) 4 times and 2dc], 2dc into each of next 2sps; repeat from * to end, omitting the last 4dc. Fasten off.

EDGE No 7.

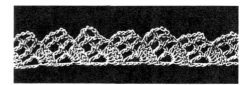

Make 10ch.

Row 1. 1tr into 6th ch from hook, 1ch, miss 1ch, 1tr into next ch, 1ch, miss 1ch, into last ch work (1tr 1ch and 1tr), 4ch, turn.

Row 2. Miss first tr, (1tr into next tr, 1ch) twice, 1tr into next tr, 5tr into last sp, 5ch, turn.

Row 3. 1tr into first tr, (1ch, miss 1tr, 1tr into next tr) twice, 1ch, 1tr into next sp, 4ch, turn.

Repeat rows 2 and 3 for length required. Fasten off.

MOTIFS

Motifs are small patterned circles, squares or other shapes, which when joined together form larger pieces of crocheting. The size of the motif will vary with the size of the yarn used, see examples on page 25.

The most common motif is the Granny square. This is usually crocheted with 8ply yarn in a variety of colours and joined together to form knee rugs. This is a good way to use up scrap yarn.

GRANNY SQUARE MOTIF

Samples shown use 4ply cotton crocheted with a 2.5mm hook, and #10 cotton crocheted with a 1.75mm hook.

Make 5ch, and join with a sl st to form a ring.

Round 1. 3ch, 2tr into the ring, (2ch, 3tr into the ring) 3 times, 2ch, sl st into the 3rd ch of the beginning 3ch. (4 groups of 3tr separated by 2ch)

4ply cotton

and

#10 cotton

Round 2. Sl st across the next 2tr and into the 2ch space, 3ch, (2tr 2ch 3tr) into the same space, * 1ch, miss 3tr, (3tr 2ch 3tr) into the next 2ch space; repeat from * twice more, 1ch, miss 3tr, sl st into the 3rd ch of the beginning 3ch.
(4 groups of 3tr 2ch 3tr separated by 1ch)

Round 3. Sl st across the next 2tr and into the 2ch space, 3ch, (2tr 2ch 3tr) into the same space, * 1ch, miss 3tr, 3tr in next 1ch space, 1ch, miss 3tr, (3tr 2ch 3tr) into the next 2ch space; repeat from * twice more, 1ch, miss 3tr, 3tr in next 1ch space, 1ch, sl st into the 3rd ch of

the beginning 3ch. (4 groups of 3tr 2ch 3tr separated by 1ch 3tr 1ch)

25

Round 4. Sl st across the next 2tr and into the 2ch space, 3ch, (2tr 2ch 3tr) into the same space, * (1ch, miss 3tr, 3tr in next 1ch space) twice, 1ch, miss 3tr, (3tr 2ch 3tr) into the next 2ch space; repeat from * twice more, (1ch, miss 3tr, 3tr in next 1ch space) twice, 1ch, sl st into the 3rd ch of the beginning 3ch. (4 groups of 3tr 2ch 3tr separated by 1ch 3tr 1ch 3tr 1ch.) Fasten off.

Variation: Use a different colour for each round.

FLOWER MOTIF

Using #10 cotton crocheted with a 1.75mm hook will make a motif 7.5cm in diameter as shown opposite.

Using #20 cotton crocheted with a 1.25mm hook will make a motif 6cm in diameter.

FIRST MOTIF
Commence with 8ch, join with a sl st to form a ring.

Round 1. Into the ring work 18dc, join with a sl st into the first dc.

Round 2. 3ch, miss next 2dc, 1tr in next dc, * 2ch, 1tr into same place as last tr, 2ch, leaving the last loop of each st on the hook, work 1tr in same place as last tr, miss next 2dc, 1tr in next dc, thread over and draw thread through all the loops on the hook (a joint treble made); repeat from * working second half of last joint tr into same place as sl st in round 1, 2ch, 1tr into same place, 2ch, sl st into the first tr. (6 groups of 1tr 2ch joint tr 2ch)

Round 3. 5ch, 5triptr into same place as sl st, * 3ch, leaving the last loop of each st on hook, work 3tr into next tr, thread over and draw the thread through all the loops on the hook (a 3tr cluster made), 3ch, 6triptr into next joint tr; repeat from * omitting 6triptr at end of last repeat, join with a sl st into the 5th ch of the beginning 5ch. (6 groups of 3ch cluster 3ch 6triptr)

Round 4. * 6ch, work a 4triptr cluster over next 4triptr, 6ch, sl st into next triptr, 4ch, miss (3ch the 3tr cluster and 3ch), sl st into next triptr; repeat from * to end, sl st into the same place as the beginning sl st at the end of the last repeat.

(6 groups of 6ch 4triptr cluster 6ch sl st 4ch) Fasten off.

SECOND and FOLLOWING MOTIFS

When working more than one motif, work second motif as for first motif for 3 rounds then join as follows in round 4.

Round 4. 6ch, work a 4triptr cluster over next 4triptr, **sl st into the corresponding ch of the first motif,** 6ch, sl st into the next triptr on the second motif, 4ch, sl st into the next triptr, **6ch, sl st into corresponding ch on next petal of first motif,** 4triptr cluster over next 4triptr on second motif and complete as for first motif.

27

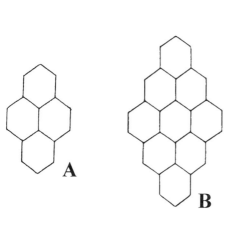

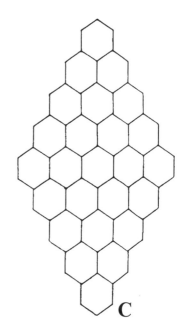

Fig 45

FLOWER MOTIF
DRESSING TABLE SET

Materials
3 (20g) balls #10 or #20 cotton

Using the diagrams in Fig 45 above as a guide, join the motifs to form a 3 piece dressing table set.

If using #10 cotton make 2 of A (ea approx 15 x 20cm) and 1 of B (approx 22.5 x 34.5cm).

If using # 20 cotton make 2 of B (ea approx 16 x 24cm) and 1 of C (approx 26.5 x 44cm)

ENVELOPE PURSE in shell stitch

Size - 22cm wide

Materials
3 (20g) balls #10 crochet cotton
1.50mm crochet hook
25cm of lining material
23cm zip and a button

Starting at the top (inside of purse) make 85ch.

Row 1. 2tr in the 4th ch from the hook, (counting the turning ch as 1tr), * miss 2ch, 1dc in next ch, miss 2ch, 5tr in next ch (shell made); repeat from * to end, ending row with miss 2ch, 1dc in last ch, turn. (13½ shells)

Row 2. 3ch, 2tr in last dc made in previous row, * miss 2tr of next shell, 1dc in next tr, 5tr in next dc; repeat from * to end, ending row with 1dc between last tr of half shell and turning ch, turn.

Repeat row 2 until piece measures 34cm in length. Fasten off.

Lay the crocheted piece on top of the lining and cut around the edge. Sew the lining to the crocheted piece. Sew one side of the zipper across one short end on the lining side. Cut another piece of lining slightly larger than the crocheted piece and place over the first lining. Fold into an envelope shape with the wrong side out and sew the sides neatly. Turn right side out, open the zipper and sew into place.

BUTTON LOOP Make 13ch, turn. Sl st into the 2nd ch from hook and into each ch to end. Fasten off. Sew ends of this chain at centre of flap to make a loop for the button. Sew on a button to correspond with button loop.

ROUND DOILY

Size:
27cm diameter

Materials
15g of #40 crochet cotton
1.00mm crochet hook

Tension:
First 4 rounds measure 6.5cm in diameter.

Make 12ch and join with a sl st to form a ring.

Round 1. 3ch, 23tr into the ring, join with sl st to 3rd of the beginning 3ch. (24tr)

Round 2. 9ch, * miss 1tr, 1dtr into next tr, 5ch; repeat from * to end, ending last repeat with a sl st into the 4th ch of the beginning 9ch. (12 loops)

Round 3. Into each 5ch loop work (1dc 1htr 3tr 1htr and 1dc), sl st into the beginning dc.

Round 4. Sl st to centre tr of group, 1dc into centre tr, * 9ch, sl st into the 5th ch from the hook, 3ch, 7tr into loop just made, 3ch, sl st into base of 5ch loop, 4ch, 1dc into centre tr at next loop; repeat from * to end, omitting 1dc at end of last repeat, sl st into the beginning dc. (12 rings of 3ch 7tr 3ch separated by 4ch 1dc) Break off yarn.

Round 5. Attach yarn with a sl st to centre tr on any ring, * 11ch, 1dc into centre tr of next ring; repeat from * to end, ending with 11ch, sl st into same place as beginning sl st. (12 loops)

Round 6. 3ch, * 1tr into each of next 5ch, 3tr into centre ch, 1tr into each of next 5ch, 1tr into next dc; repeat from * to end, join with sl st into 3rd ch of the beginning 3ch. (168tr)

Round 7. Sl st into each of next 6tr, 3ch, 1tr into each of next 2tr, * 11ch, 1tr into each tr of next 3tr group; repeat from * to end, ending with 11ch, sl st into 3rd ch of the beginning 3ch. (12 groups of 3tr separated by 11ch)

Round 8. 3ch, 1tr into same place as sl st, * 1tr into next tr, 2tr into next tr, 7ch, 1dc into next loop, 7ch, 2tr into next tr; repeat from * to end, ending with 7ch, sl st into 3rd ch of the beginning 3ch. (12 groups of 5tr separated by 7ch 1dc 7ch)

Round 9. 3ch, * 1tr into each of next 4tr, (5ch, 1dc into next loop) twice, 5ch, 1tr into next tr; repeat from * to end, omitting 1tr at end of last repeat, sl st into 3rd ch of the beginning 3ch. (12 groups of 5tr separated by 5ch 1dc 5ch 1dc 5ch)

Round 10. 3ch, 1tr into each of next 4tr, * 9ch, 1dc into centre loop, 9ch, 1tr into each of next 5tr; repeat from * to end, omitting 5tr at end of last repeat, sl st into 3rd ch of the beginning 3ch. (12 groups of 5tr separated by 9ch 1dc 9ch)

Round 11. 3ch, 1tr into each of next 4tr, * 5ch, 1dc into next loop, 9ch, 1dc into next loop, 5ch, 1tr into each of next 5tr; repeat from * to end, omitting 5tr at end of last repeat, sl st into 3rd ch of the beginning 3ch. (12 groups of 5tr separated by 5ch 1dc 9ch 1dc 5ch)

Round 12. 3ch, 1tr into each of next 4tr, * 7ch, 1dc into centre loop, 7ch, 1tr into each of next 5tr; repeat from * to end, omitting 5tr at end of last repeat, sl st into 3rd ch of the beginning 3ch. (12 groups of 5tr separated by 7ch 1dc 7ch)

Round 13. 3ch, 1tr into each of next 4tr, * 5ch, 1dc into next loop, 9ch, 1dc into next loop, 5ch, 1tr into each of next 5tr; repeat from * to end, omitting 5tr at end of last repeat, sl st into 3rd ch of the beginning 3ch. (12 groups of 5tr separated by 5ch 1dc 9ch 1dc 5ch)

Round 14. 3ch, 1tr into each of next 4tr, * 8ch, 1dc into centre loop, 8ch, 1tr into each of next 5tr; repeat from * to end, omitting 5tr at end of last repeat, sl st into 3rd ch of the beginning 3ch. (12 groups of 5tr separated by 8ch 1dc 8ch)

Round 15. 3ch, 1tr into each of next 4tr, * 7ch, 5dtr into next dc, 7ch, 1tr into each of next 5tr; repeat from * to end, omitting 5tr at end of

last repeat, sl st into 3rd ch of the beginning 3ch. (12 groups of 5tr separated by 7ch 5dtr 7ch)

Round 16. 3ch, 1tr into each of next 4tr, * 2ch, 1tr into next sp, 9ch, leaving the last loop of each st on the hook, 1dtr into each of next 5dtr, thread over and draw through all loops on hook (a 5dtr cluster made), 9ch, 1tr into next sp, 2ch, 1tr into each of next 5tr; repeat from * to end, omitting 5tr at end of last repeat, sl st into 3rd ch of the beginning 3ch. (12 groups of 5tr separated by 2ch 1tr 9ch cluster 9ch 1tr 2ch)

Round 17. 3ch, 1tr into each of next 4tr, * 2ch, 1tr into next tr, 2ch, into next loop work [1tr 3ch 1tr], 3ch, into next loop work [1tr 3ch 1tr], 2ch, 1tr into next tr, 2ch, 1tr into each of next 5tr; repeat from * to end, omitting 5tr at end of last repeat, sl st into 3rd ch of the beginning 3ch. (12 groups of 5tr separated by 2ch 1tr 2ch [1tr 3ch 1tr] 3ch [1tr 3ch 1tr] 2ch 1tr 2ch)

Round 18. 3ch, 1tr into next tr, * into next tr work (1tr 2ch and 1tr), 1tr into each of next 2tr, 1ch, 1tr into next tr, 2ch, 1tr into next tr, [3ch, 1tr into next tr] 3 times, 2ch, 1tr into next tr, 1ch, 1tr into each of next 2tr; repeat from * to end, omitting 2tr at end of last repeat, sl st into 3rd ch of the beginning 3ch. (12 groups of 3tr 2ch 3tr separated by 1ch 1tr 2ch 1tr [3ch 1tr] 3 times, 2ch 1tr 1ch)

Round 19. 4ch, 1dtr into each of next 2tr, * 2ch, 1dtr into space, 2ch, 1dtr into each of next 3tr, 3ch, miss 1tr, 1dtr into next tr, 3ch, 1dtr into next tr, 3dtr into next sp, 1dtr into next tr, 3ch, 1dtr into next tr, 3ch, miss 1tr, 1dtr into each of next 3tr; repeat from * to end, omitting 3dtr at end of last repeat, sl st into 4th ch of the beginning 4ch. (12 groups of 3dtr 2ch 1dtr 2ch 3dtr separated by 3ch 1dtr 3ch 5dtr 3ch 1dtr 3ch)

Round 20. 4ch, 1dtr into each of next 2dtr, * [3ch, 1dtr into next sp] twice, 3ch, 1dtr into each of next 3dtr, 1ch, 1tr into next dtr, 5ch, 1dc into centre dtr of next dtr group, 5ch, 1tr into next dtr, 1ch, 1dtr into each of next 3dtr; repeat from * to end, omitting 3dtr at end of last repeat, sl st into 4th ch of the beginning 4ch. (12 groups of 3tr [3ch and 1dtr] twice, 3ch and 3dtr separated by 1ch 1tr 5ch 1dc 5ch 1tr 1ch)

Round 21. 4ch, 1dtr into each of next 2dtr, * [5ch, 1dtr into next sp] 3 times, 5ch, 1dtr into each of next 3dtr, 3ch, miss next sp, 1dc into next loop, 7ch, 1dc into next loop,

3ch, 1dtr into each of next 3dtr; repeat from * to end, omitting 3dtr at end of last repeat, sl st into 4th ch of the beginning 4ch. (12 groups of 3dtr [5ch and 1dtr] 3 times 5ch 3dtr separated by 3ch 1dc 7ch 1dc 3ch)

Round 22. 3ch, 1tr into each of next 2dtr, * 6tr into each of next 4 loops, 1tr into each of next 3dtr, 5ch, 1dc into centre loop, 5ch, 1tr into each of the next 3dtr; repeat from * to end, omitting 3tr at end of last repeat, sl st into 3rd ch of the beginning 3ch. (12 groups of 30tr separated by 5ch 1dc 5ch)

Round 23. 5ch, leaving the last loop of each on hook, 2triptr into same place as last sl st, thread over and draw through all loops on hook (a cluster made), * (5ch, miss 2tr, a 3triptr cluster into next tr) 9 times, 5ch, miss 1tr, a 3triptr cluster into last tr, miss (5ch 1dc 5ch), a 3triptr cluster into first tr of next tr group; repeat from * omitting a 3triptr cluster at end of last repeat, sl st into top of beginning cluster. (12 groups of [cluster and 5ch] 10 times cluster)

Round 24. Sl st to centre of next 5ch, * 8ch, sl st into 5th ch from hook (picot made), 3ch, 1dc into next loop, repeat from * to end, sl st into the beginning sl st. (12 groups of [3ch picot 3ch 1dc] 10 times). End off.

WASHING INSTRUCTIONS

Wash in warm soapy water, rinse well, roll in a towel to remove excess water, dry flat and iron into shape on the reverse side of the work while still damp, starching with spray starch if necessary.

MOTIF TABLE CENTRE

Materials
1 (50g) ball #20 crochet cotton
1.25mm crochet hook

Motif measures: 4cm
Centre measures: 39cm x 23cm

First Motif
Make 12ch and join with a sl st to form a ring.

Round 1. 1ch, into ring work 24dc, sl st into the beginning dc. (24dc)

Round 2. 4ch, leaving the last loop of each st on the hook, work 2dtr into same place as sl st, yarn over hook and draw it through all 3 loops on hook (cluster made), * 5ch, miss 1dc, leaving the last loop of each st on the hook, work 3dtr into next dc, yarn over hook and draw it through all 4 loops on hook (another cluster); repeat from * ending with 5ch, sl st the into top of first cluster. (12 clusters each separated by 5ch)

Round 3. Sl st across each of next 2ch, 1dc into same loop, * 5ch, into next loop work (a 3dtr cluster 7ch and a 3dtr cluster), [5ch, 1dc into next loop] twice; repeat from * omitting 1dc at end of last repeat, sl st into the beginning dc. (4 groups of cluster 7ch cluster separated by 5ch 1dc 5ch 1dc 5ch) Break off.

Second Motif

Work rounds 1 and 2 as for first motif.

Round 3. Sl st into each of next 2ch, 1dc into loop, 5ch, 1 cluster into next loop, 3ch, **sl st into corresponding corner loop on first motif,** 3ch, 1 cluster in same loop as last cluster on second motif, **(2ch, sl st into next loop on first motif,** 2ch, 1dc into next loop on second motif) twice, **2ch, sl st into next loop on first motif,** 2ch, 1 cluster into next loop of second motif, **3ch, sl st into next loop on first motif,** 3ch, 1 cluster into same loop as last cluster on second motif, (5ch, 1dc into next loop) twice on second motif, and complete as for first motif from * to end.

Make 5 rows of 9 motifs, joining them as second motif was joined to first motif (where 4 corners meet, sl st 3rd and 4th corners to joining sl st of the previous 2 corners).

Table centre edging

Round 1. Attach the yarn to any free corner loop, 4ch and complete a cluster in same loop, 5ch, 1 cluster into same loop, * 5ch, 1dc into next 5ch loop, 5ch, into next loop work (1 cluster, 5ch, 1 cluster), 5ch, 1dc into next loop, 5ch, into joining space of motifs work (1 cluster 5ch and 1 cluster); repeat from * to end, *making 1 cluster 5ch and 1 cluster into each corner loop,* and ending last repeat 5ch, sl st into top of the beginning cluster.

Round 2. Sl st into corner loop, 4ch and complete cluster, (5ch and 1 cluster into same place) twice, * 5ch, 1dc into next loop, 2ch, 1dc into next loop, 5ch, into next loop work (1 cluster 5ch and 1 cluster); repeat from * to end, *making (1 cluster, 5ch) twice and 1 cluster into each corner loop,* ending last repeat 5ch, sl st into the beginning cluster. Fasten off.

THE WILLOW STORY

Materials
65g #10 crochet cotton
1.50mm crochet hook

Size: 58cm x 31cm (90 blocks wide x 66 rows high)

Tension: 15½ spaces to 10cm
21 rows to 10cm

space (sp): 2ch, miss 2sts, 1tr in next st.
block (blk): 3tr.
beginning block: 3ch, miss 1tr, 1tr into each of the next 3sts.

Make 274ch.

Row 1. 1tr into the 5th ch from hook, 1tr into each ch to end, turn. (271tr)

Row 2. 3ch, miss 1tr, 1tr in each of the next 3tr [beginning block made], 1tr in each of the next 3tr [another block made], 2ch, miss 2tr, 1tr in next tr [1 space made], work (1 block and 1 space) to last 3tr, 1tr in each tr [block], turn. (beginning blk, blk, [space, block] 44 times)

Row 3. 3ch, miss 1tr, 1tr into each of the next 3tr [beginning block], 1tr in each st to last 6sts, work (1 space and 1 block) in these sts, turn. (beg blk, 87blks, 1sp, 1blk)

Row 4. Beginning block, 3 blocks, 29 spaces, 8 blocks, 2 spaces, 1 block, 3 spaces, (1 block and 1 space) 4 times, 1 block, 31 spaces, 1 block, 1 space and 1 block, turn.

Continue in this manner, (working a beginning block at the beginning of every row), following the graph from row 5 until row 66 is completed. Fasten off.

Row 66

274ch

Row 1
Row 5

36